Reduce

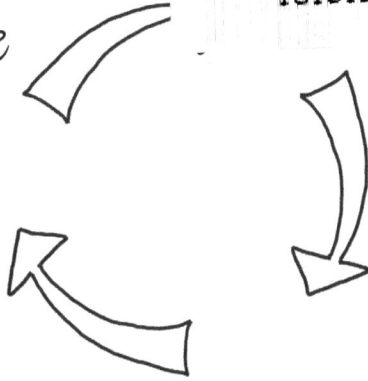

Reuse

Recycle

Inspiring young authors to write and imagine.

First edition January 2020

www.BindingTales.com

This book was

written and illustrated by:

_____

_____

year

With a little inspiration from Binding Tales.
Always make time to read, write, and create ~ together.

creating your Book

You're going to love every step of creating your Binding Tales storybook! Here are a few pointers to help guide you in the right direction.

Tip #1
Start by reading through the entire book with an adult. This will help you think about how the story will unfold as you are writing and drawing pictures.

Tip #2
Use our free coloring sheets for practice sketching and coloring. Printed sheets can downloaded at bindingtales.com/freebies.

Tip #3
Ask questions (especially if you get stuck) and work together. Working together as a team adds to the fun!

Tip #4
The paper in your book works best with pencils, crayons and colored pencils.

Tip #5
Be creative and have fun, there's no limit to your imagination.

Tip #6
Inspire others with your masterpiece! Take a picture while you show off your favorite pages of the finished book and tag @BindingTales on social media!

Co-authoring a book is something to be very proud of!
GREAT job! *We're proud of you!*

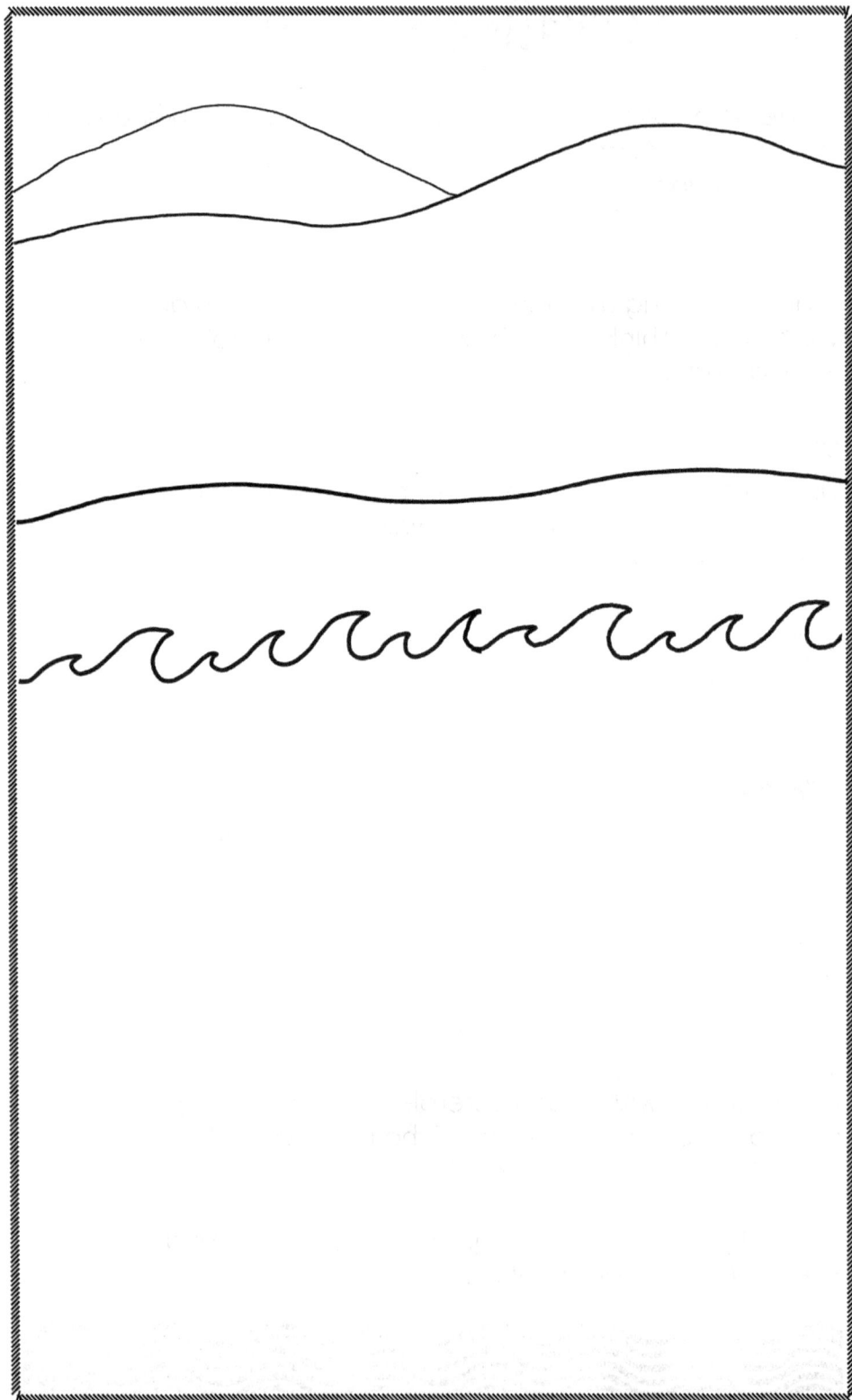

The planet Earth is

_____

_____

_____

On land there are a lot of

_____

_____

_____

The oceans are filled with

_____

_____

_____

The planet Earth is awesome because

_____

_____

_____

_____

The Earth gets boo-boos when

_____

_____

_____

_____

But I can help!

A lot of things in my house run on

_____

Some things I can turn OFF when
they are not being used are:

_____

_____

_____

_____

Not wasting our resources is called

C

_____

Example: Turning off the lights will

_____

I use water for many things, including:

_____

_____

_____

_____

If the water stays running while I

_____

a lot of fresh water will be

_____

I can **CONSERVE** water by

_____

_____

_____

Three important verbs for helping Earth are:

R _____

R _____

R _____

Reducing means that I

_____

_____

_____

It is very helpful to reduce my use of

_____

because _____

_____

Recycling is when

_____

_____

_____

I can recycle lots of things!
I can help my family recycle by

_____

_____

_____

_____

Recycling makes me feel

_____

_____

When I outgrow my clothes I can

_____

_____

I grow very _____

I need bigger clothes about every

_____

_____

I imagine my old clothes are now

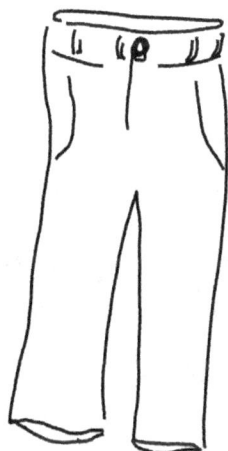

_____

_____

_____

_____

Feeding my unused fruits and vegetables
back into the soil is called

_____

Some people have a compost pile on the

_____

Other people put compost inside a

_____

I can compost

_____

_____

It is very helpful to plant more

_____

Trees produce_____

Protecting the trees around us is called

_____

_____

In my house we store food in

_____

_____

_____

To reduce waste, I can pack my
snacks and lunch for school inside

_____

_____

_____

Reducing waste makes me feel

_____

_____

There are lots of ways I can help

_____

_____

Three things I will start doing now are

_____

_____

_____

One BIG change my family and
I will work on together is

_____

_____

_____

Binding Tales

Welcome to Binding Tales, bound paperback books that inspire and guide young authors with guided composition and illustration prompts to create their very own storybooks!

Your child's imagination has poured onto these pages, instantly preserving their priceless creation for you to cherish forever. *How cool is that?*

Our hope is that Binding Tales helps your family capture and create memories of your own. As our library of books grows, we would be honored to share in the growth of your young author!

Your Creativity Co-Contributors,

The Binding Tales Family

Hillary, Adam, Eva & Tyler Dow

Why stop with one? Once your young author catches the writer's itch they'll want to keep going! Browse and buy from our children's book store at bindingtales.com, or add books to your cart on Amazon. www.**amazon.com/author/hillarydow**

Thank you!
· FOR YOUR SUPPORT ·

REQUEST

Thank you for creating your very own Binding Tales book!

It would mean the world to me if you would take a short minute to leave a review on Google, as your kind feedback is much appreciated and so very important. Thank you very much for your support and valuable time!

Hillary

https://qrco.de/BTGoogleReview